THE HOW-TO-MAKE-A-BOOK BOOK

W9-BDE-476

Grades 1-6

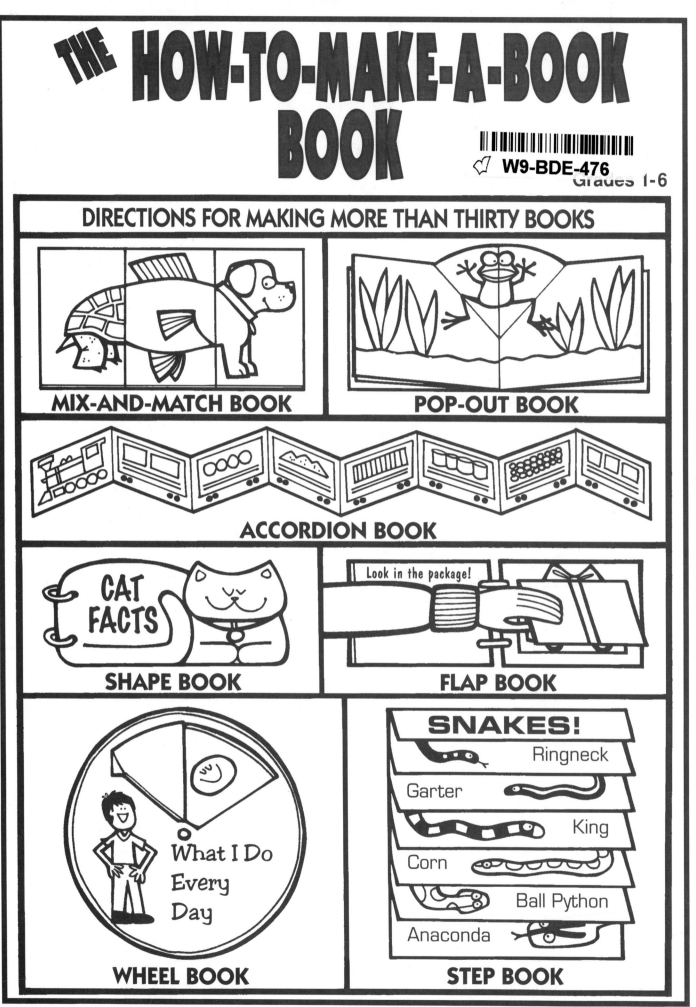

DIRECTIONS FOR MAKING MORE THAN THIRTY BOOKS

MIX-AND-MATCH BOOK

POP-OUT BOOK

ACCORDION BOOK

CAT FACTS

SHAPE BOOK

Look in the package!

FLAP BOOK

What I Do Every Day

WHEEL BOOK

SNAKES!

Ringneck
Garter
King
Corn
Ball Python
Anaconda

STEP BOOK

Written by Cynthia Costello • Illustrated by Bev Armstrong

The Learning Works

Written by
Cynthia Costello

Illustrated by
Bev Armstrong

Editing and Page Design by
Clark Editorial & Design

Introduction

Making books is a creative way for children to express themselves through words and pictures. In this book, you will find step-by-step instructions for making thirty different kinds of individualized books, as well as a variety of suggestions for fun book themes. Children can use these instructions and ideas to create their own library of original books filled with special memories that will last for years. Personalized books also make great gifts for any special occasion.

Each project includes a list of supplies children will need and a set of illustrated directions. A section called *Teacher's Corner* accompanies every book-making project and contains an annotated list of books and creative ideas. Teachers will find it helpful to read these sections before beginning each project.

Although this book has been written for teachers and students, the projects are also fun and easy to make at home with children. Simply set up a work table, gather the necessary supplies, and follow the directions for any of the book ideas you like.

We planted a long row of seeds in the soft brown dirt. Then I watered them, using my big new watering can.

SUNFLOWER

GLUE

3

Contents

Contents

▪ Teacher/Parent Resources ▪

Book-Making Center and Project Guidelines

Set up a book-making center with the necessary supplies in a convenient location in your classroom. Have students work at their desks for individual projects, and arrange seating at tables for three to four students for group projects. As a class project, you may wish to create a poster that briefly lists the basic steps for all projects (see below).

Supplies Needed

- heavyweight construction paper or tagboard in assorted colors for book covers (or a supply of pre-made covers)
- tagboard scraps
- scratch paper
- white drawing paper
- lined writing paper
- parchment paper (for scroll book)
- stapler
- hole punch
- ruler
- yarn or narrow ribbon
- manila envelopes
- paper fasteners

- masking tape
- clear tape
- crayons
- felt-tipped markers and pens
- pencils
- scissors
- white glue
- glue stick
- craft knife (adult supervision is needed during use)
- loose-leaf rings
- laminator (for selected projects)
- assortment of craft items (for texture book)
- craft sticks (for slot book)

Basic Steps for All Projects

1. Listen to an explanation of the project. (If possible, provide students with a sample of the book.)
2. Organize your materials and decide what type of book to make.
3. Put your thoughts on scratch paper.
4. Proofread your work for clarity, spelling, and punctuation. (Younger children can ask a teacher or class aide to check their work.)
5. Use a dictionary or word-bank list to check spelling. (Assume a younger child will use invented spelling.)
6. Get feedback from a teacher, an aide, or a classmate before creating a finished version.
7. Make a neat, finished project to bind in a cover.

Getting Started and Staying Organized

Helping Children Who Do Not Read

Young children will need a teacher or classroom aide to write their stories as they dictate them. Pairing an older student with a younger "book buddy" also works well. The older student meets with his or her book buddy and writes down the story dictated by the younger child. The older student then supervises the book buddy in making one of the suggested books based on the story. When it's finished, the older student reads the book to his or her book buddy and gives the book to the younger child.

Helping Older Children Get Started

Older children who can work independently will sometimes need help with story ideas. You can suggest they write in response to a favorite read-aloud story or respond to a story they have already read in one of the following ways:

- Rewrite the story with themselves as one of the main characters.
- Make up a sequel to the story.
- Use a diary format to recount important events in the story.
- Change the characters or setting of the original story, or invent a new ending.
- Make up a story using their favorite character from a story they have already read.
- Adapt the characters and/or setting of the story to a book about numbers, letters, shapes or colors.
- Show the sequence of the story with a clock face on each page.
- Research and write about a nonfiction topic related to the story.
- Make a book using a poem or song they have written based on the story.

Ideas for Staying Organized

Post the directions for each book-making project in a convenient location in the classroom, or photocopy the directions for each type of book and put them in a binder students can use at the book-making center.

If possible, have a completed sample of each kind of book on display.

Create student files for work in progress to keep projects neatly organized and easy to find.

Assign older students the tasks of keeping the materials in order and putting them away after each class.

With these suggestions, you and your students are ready to experience the fun and rewards of book making. So choose a project you like and get started!

7

Accordion Book

What You Need

- ten pieces of colored construction paper (9" x 12")
- train patterns from page 82 (if making a train book)
- scratch paper
- scissors
- glue
- crayons
- felt-tipped markers
- pencils
- clear tape
- two narrow ribbons (24" long)

What You Do

1. An accordion book unfolds to make a long string of pictures. Think of something long that would be fun to make, such as a row of elephants linked trunk to tail, a string of cars or trucks, or a train. If you want to make a train, you can use the patterns on page 82 to make one engine and seven cars. If you choose another idea, you can make different patterns and follow the same steps as those for the train book.

2. Cut out the cars and engine. Glue the engine to the bottom half of a 9" x 12" piece of construction paper, as shown. Do the same for the train cars. Arrange the cars in the order you like and stack them with the engine on the top. Write a story, draw pictures, or do both on your train cars. It's a good idea to write your story on scratch paper first, so you can make any changes you want before you put it on your train.

Accordion Book

3. Fold each sheet of the paper back and down and glue it shut. Allow your pages to dry. Arrange the cars side by side in story order. Tape the pages to each other along the short (six-inch) sides—both front and back. You will have a long train!

4. Fold the pages back and forth in an accordion pattern until the book is closed.

5. Make front and back covers by folding two sheets of colored construction paper in half. Decorate the front cover and print the title of the story on it. Place a ribbon in the middle of each cover, as shown in the diagram. Glue the ribbon in place. Glue the folded paper shut over the ribbon to make the covers strong. Tape the covers to the book as you did for the train cars. (Do not tape over the ribbon. Just tape up to it, leave a space, and continue taping on the other side of it.) Tie the finished book closed with the ends of the ribbon.

Teacher's Corner

- ***The Polar Express*** by Chris Van Allsburg (Houghton Mifflin, 1985)
Your kids can make a class book based on this Caldecott Medal winner. Distribute the train cars, and assign each person part of the story to illustrate. For a special effect, provide foil to highlight Santa's bell, which is central to the story. Children can also make the book in alternating pages of red and green for a Christmas theme or with dark blue paper for the story's nighttime setting.

- ***Hey! Get Off Our Train*** by John Burningham (Crown, 1989)
In this book, a young boy dreams he saves endangered animals by taking them aboard his toy train. Students can write their own versions of the story and illustrate their train cars with their favorite animals. Some children might want to retell the story using a white, cloud-shaped motif to indicate dreaming. In this case, they can glue train patterns to cut-outs of white, puffy clouds instead of colored-paper rectangles. Otherwise, they should follow the same directions provided for the accordion train book.

- ***Do You Want to Be My Friend?*** by Eric Carle (Harper Collins, 1971)
Children will enjoy this story of a little mouse's efforts to find a friend. Across the bottom of each page, the reader sees a portion of an outstretched snake. The mouse and a variety of animals appear at the top. Kids will have fun writing and illustrating their own version of this mouse tale using an accordion-book format.

The How-To-Make-a-Book Book
© The Learning Works, Inc.

Almanac

An **almanac** is a book containing information on many subjects, including politics, weather, sports, science, and world events. Some almanacs provide information about one subject only. For example, an almanac on astronomy might contain facts about stars, planets, tides, eclipses, and satellites.

For this project, three to five students can make a group almanac.

What You Need

- several sheets of lined writing paper ($8\frac{1}{2}$" x 11") and white drawing paper ($8\frac{1}{2}$" x 11"), or writing paper patterns on pages 84-85
- two pieces of colored tagboard for the cover (9" x 12")
- crayons or felt-tipped markers
- pencils
- scissors
- glue
- stapler
- masking tape

What You Do

1. Decide what information your group wants to include in an almanac. Choose a subject you are studying in school that interests the group. For example, if you are learning about weather, you could research topics such as acid rain, cloud seeding, and flood control.

2. Each person in the group chooses a topic to research and write about. Each person should give his or her report a title. Put the individual reports together for a first draft of your group almanac. Check the spelling, punctuation, and grammar. Make any changes that are needed.

3. Each person then writes and signs a final copy of his or her work on lined paper. Illustrate the final version with drawings, cutouts of pictures, or other designs.

4. Put the individual pages in alphabetical order by title, and create a table of contents.

Almanac

5. Make a hinged cover by cutting an inch-wide strip off the long side of each piece of tagboard. Join the pieces together again using masking tape, as shown. The tape will be on the inside of the finished book. To complete your book, stack the pages between the front and back covers. Staple the book together along the strip. Decorate your cover.

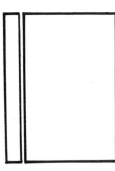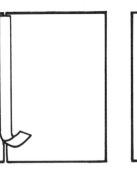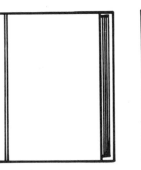

Teacher's Corner

In 1732, Benjamin Franklin began writing and printing *Poor Richard's Almanac*. It was filled with interesting facts, useful information for farmers, and clever sayings that we remember today. A few of these proverbs are:

Early to bed, early to rise, makes a man healthy, wealthy, and wise.
Haste makes waste.
Great talkers, little doers.
A true friend is the best possession.
No gains without pains.

Make sure your students understand the meaning of each proverb. Challenge them to write their own sayings or copy those they like on several pages of their almanacs.

■ *Dear Benjamin Banneker* by Andrea Davis Pinkney (Harcourt, Brace, Jovanovich, 1994)
Banneker was the first African American to write an almanac. He did his own research and included information about weather, planting, and astronomy. You can share this account of his life with your students and show them examples of more recent almanacs.

■ *And Now . . . The Weather* by Anita Ganeri (Aladdin Books, 1992)
Consider using this book to introduce a project for making a weather almanac. Among other things, students can include a graph of daily temperatures, a chart of humidity and precipitation, and information about emergency weather conditions. For more ideas, suggest they watch televised weather forecasts and, if possible, arrange for a local meteorologist to visit the class!

■ *Macmillan's Illustrated Almanac for Kids* (Macmillan, 1981)
■ *The Macmillan Book of Fascinating Facts* (Macmillan, 1989)
■ *The Information Please Kids' Almanac* (Houghton Mifflin, 1992)
These books are excellent examples of the almanac format. They are easy to read and have lots of information of interest to children.

Banner Book

What You Need

- five sheets of white paper (11" x 14")
- one piece of construction paper for the cover (12" x 18")
- crayons or felt-tipped markers
- pencils
- scissors
- stapler
- laminator (optional)

What You Do

1. In a banner book the large center pages fold out to the sides, as shown in the illustration. This makes a large space for drawing pictures, maps, or charts.

   Since the center of the book folds out, it is necessary to organize all of the pages first. For a twelve-page book with a fold-out center, you need five 11" x 14" sheets of paper. Fold them in half, as shown in the diagram.

2. Use one sheet of paper to make the fold-out center section. Cut one inch off both eleven-inch sides of the paper and discard the small pieces. Cut the large piece that remains through the center, as shown. Tape these two pieces neatly to the outer edges of the center page of your book. They should fold in without touching at the center. The fold-out section is perfect for a time line, panorama, or treasure map.

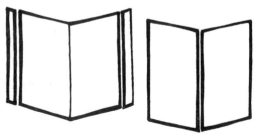
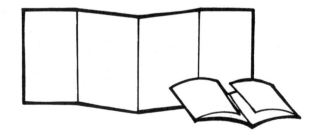

Banner Book

3. Sketch in your story and pictures. Then check your work and make any changes that are needed. Color the drawings.

4. Line up all the pages along the fold and join at the center with one staple.

5. Fold the construction paper in half to form a cover. Fit it around your finished pages. Decorate your cover and ask an adult to laminate it, if possible. Attach the cover by stapling the pages securely through the center. When you are attaching the cover, be careful not to staple the fold-out section.

Teacher's Corner

■ *Macmillan Children's Guide to Dinosaurs and Other Prehistoric Animals* by Philip Whitfield (Macmillan, 1992)

This book has renderings of dinosaurs living in natural settings. The fold-out pages display panoramic scenes, which students can use for ideas for their own books. One way students can organize their books is to write information about their favorite dinosaurs on every page except the last, which they reserve to explain theories of extinction.

■ *Just Us Women* by Jeanette Caines (Harper Trophy, 1982)

Share this modern account of a girl and her aunt traveling to North Carolina. Students can then write about a real or imagined trip with their own relative(s). Ask them to draw a map of their route on the fold-out sections of their books. This project provides students with an opportunity to practice their geography, map reading, and writing skills.

■ *Things That Go* by Anne Rockwell (Dutton, 1986)

Students can make time lines for a variety of themes, including transportation. Suggest that they trace the history of transportation or the development of a specific form of transportation in a fold-out time line. This book also contains information about inventors of new forms of transportation. Students can use this information to enhance their time lines.

■ *People* by Peter Spier (Doubleday, 1980)

This book, which celebrates diversity, is a springboard for any multicultural unit. For example, students can make books containing information about different countries. Ask them to include the flag and map for each country as well as interesting facts about its people and culture. The center fold-out section is ideal for drawings of children from all over the world wearing their native dress.

Big Book

What You Need

- several sheets of white craft paper (14" x 18")
- two pieces of colored tagboard (15" x 20")
- crayons or felt-tipped markers
- pencils
- hole punch
- ruler
- four loose-leaf rings (1" diameter)

What You Do

1. Choose a subject for your big book. Plan each page carefully. Sketch the drawings and print the words lightly.

2. Check your work and make any changes that are needed. Color the pictures.

3. Put the finished pages in order.

An elephant's tail may be five feet long. How long (tall) are you?

A giraffe is so tall that a man can walk under it.

Big Book

4. Print the title of your book on the front cover and add a picture.

5. Measure down the left side of the cover and punch holes at two inches, seven inches, thirteen inches, and eighteen inches. Using the front cover as a guide, punch holes in the back cover and inside pages. Line up all the pages and join your book together with the four loose-leaf rings.

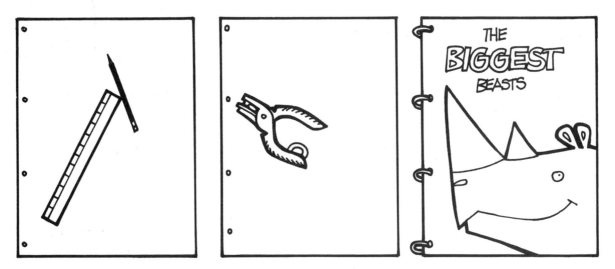

Teacher's Corner

■ *If the Dinosaurs Came Back* by Bernard Most (Harcourt, Brace, Jovanovich, 1978)
It's fun to make big books about BIG topics. This book features pictures of dinosaurs in simple shapes that are easy to copy. It is an excellent book to remake in detail with black and white line drawings of scenery and brightly-colored dinosaurs. Your students can extend the theme by creating their own uses for the dinosaurs in their big books.

■ *Swamp Angel* by Anne Isaacs (Dutton, 1994)
■ *Rude Giants* by Audrey Wood (Harcourt, Brace, Jovanovich, 1993)
Other popular BIG topics are giants and tall tales. Students can write other adventures for the "greatest woodsman in Tennessee" or make up their own stories about "gentle giants."

■ *Hey Diddle Diddle and Other Mother Goose Rhymes* by Tomie Paola (Putnam, 1985)
Check out this collection for its clever illustrations. Encourage your students to write their own poetry in conjunction with the study of word families, or make a big book with favorite nursery rhymes on each page.

Books made in big-book format are ideal for shared reading with young students. You can easily make your own set for the classroom. Choose stories that are repetitive, and illustrate them clearly so that students who do not read can enjoy looking at the pictures while others read along. Display the finished books on easels and point to the words while reading so that students can practice left-to-right eye movement.

Catalog Book

What You Need

- eight sheets of construction paper (9" x 12")
- magazines and/or catalogs
- glue or glue stick
- scissors
- hole punch
- fine-tip markers
- ruler
- four loose-leaf rings (1" diameter)
- laminator (optional)

What You Do

1. Set aside two sheets of paper for your cover.

2. Choose a subject for your catalog and decide what you would like to include on each page.

3. Make thumb tabs for your catalog pages by following the diagram below. Measure and cut away the shaded areas.

4. Cut out pictures from old magazines and catalogs, and plan out your arrangement. When you are ready, glue them to the pages. Lay them flat to dry.

Catalog Book

5. Label each thumb tab with one or two words describing what is on that page.

6. Print the title and make decorations on the finished cover. Ask an adult to laminate the cover and inside pages, if possible.

7. Measure down the left side of the cover and punch holes at one inch, four inches, seven inches, and ten inches, as shown. Using the front cover as a guide, punch holes in the back cover and inside pages. Line up all the pages and join your book together with the four loose-leaf rings.

Teacher's Corner

Students can practice sorting and classifying with these versatile books. As an example, help them organize their pages into a color catalog. Ask them to cut out magazine pictures of clothing they like and to sort them by color. When they have enough of one color to fill a page, they can arrange and glue the pictures down to make a collage. After they finish all of the pages, have them write the corresponding color word on each thumb tab.

Young students can also make clothing catalogs by cutting out and sorting pictures of clothing and gluing them onto separate pages by category, such as pants, shirts, or dresses. Help them label each thumb tab correctly.

Toy catalogs are also fun for young children to make. Kids sort and classify pictures of toys they find advertised in magazines.

Students can also use pictures of furniture advertised in magazines to group and arrange in a house-shaped catalog. Provide students with a simple house-shaped cover and sheets of blank paper, also house-shaped, for the pages of their books. Students may want to arrange the pictures of furniture by room, by type, or by style. Help students organize their books, calculate new thumb tabs, and label the pages.

Envelope Book

What You Need

- five to ten manila envelopes (9" x 12")
- white tagboard squares (6" x 6")
- two pieces of colored tagboard for the cover (10" x 13")
- scissors
- crayons
- felt-tipped markers
- pencils
- masking tape
- paper fasteners
- ruler
- hole punch

What You Do

1. An envelope book is a good place to sort and store pictures. You can make animals the theme of your book and label the envelopes *mammals*, *birds*, *fish*, *reptiles*, and *amphibians*. Or you can choose other themes such as holidays, sports, food, countries, or things to wear.

2. Collect pictures related to your subject or draw them on the tagboard squares. If you wish, label the back of each picture to practice vocabulary and spelling.

3. Write a title on each envelope that tells what is inside. Then add pictures or other decorations to the front of each envelope.

4. Cut away part of the flap of each envelope, as shown. This will make it easier to open and close the envelopes after your book is put together.

Envelope Book

5. With the flap facing toward you, measure and punch three holes down the left side of each envelope.

6. Make a hinged cover as illustrated with the Almanac (see step 5 on page 11). Punch three holes down the long side of the tagboard to match the holes in the envelopes. Stack the envelopes between the front and back covers. Join the book together with paper fasteners.

7. Sort the pictures you have drawn or collected and place them in the proper envelopes.

Teacher's Corner

The envelope book is a favorite with children, and making one is a great follow-up to a class research unit. If you are studying different countries, for example, kids can use this as a theme for their envelope books. Have your students designate one country per envelope, draw a map and flag of that country on the outside of the envelope, and write important facts about that country on cards they place inside. Later, they can use their books for test reviews.

■ *State Names, Seals, Flags, and Symbols: A Historical Guide* by Benjamin F. Shearer (Greenwood Press, 1987)
Have your students make similar books for the study of states. On the outside of each envelope, they can draw a state's flag, map, flower, and bird. Inside each envelope, they can store a card with facts they have researched about that state.

■ *Twenty Names in Art* by Alan Blackwood (Cavendish, 1988)
■ *Twenty Inventors* by Jacqueline Dineed (Cavendish, 1988)
These make excellent references for student books about famous people. Suggest that kids write about people who share a special talent or common heritage.

■ *Dinosaur Days* by Joyce Milton (Random House, 1985)
Use this book for reference. Students can label their envelopes *meat-eater* and *plant-eater* or *fly*, *walk*, and *swim*. Ask them to write general information about each category on the front of their envelopes. Then they can draw pictures of dinosaurs to sort and store in their envelopes. Have them include the name of the dinosaur and some fascinating facts about that dinosaur type.

Flap Book

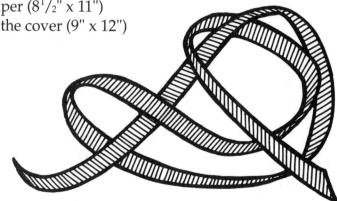

What You Need

- several sheets of white drawing paper (8½" x 11")
- two pieces of colored tagboard for the cover (9" x 12")
- crayons or felt-tipped markers
- pencils
- scissors
- glue or glue stick
- masking tape
- yarn or ribbon (24" long)
- hole punch

What You Do

1. In this book, you hide things behind flaps. The hidden things could be pictures, answers to riddles, or solutions to math problems. Plan your book so that it opens along the nine-inch side. Leave at least a one-inch margin on the left. Print the words and lightly sketch in the pictures. Decide where you will use flaps.

2. When you finish writing, color all of the pictures.

3. Cut and glue the flaps in place. If you wish, decorate the flaps.

Flap Book

4. Make a hinged cover as illustrated with the Almanac (see step 5 on page 11).

5. Punch two holes in the narrow strip on the front cover. Then use that strip as a stencil to mark where holes should be punched on the inside pages and the back cover. Punch the holes and stack the pages between the front and back covers. Tie the book together with yarn or ribbon.

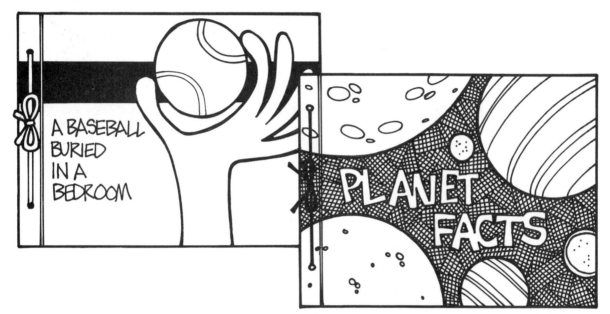

Teacher's Corner

■ *Where Is the Bear?* by Bonnie Larkin Nims (Whitman, 1988)
In this story, a young child searches his home for a favorite toy. Kids enjoy retelling this story using flaps as a tablecloth, bedspread, pillow, and other household objects. Another version of this story could involve a child looking outside his or her home for a lost pet.

■ *In the Haunted House* by Eve Bunting (Houghton Mifflin, 1990)
The reader is surprised by Halloween characters inside chests and behind doors and curtains. This book is ideal to remake in the flap-book format.

■ *Volcanoes and Earthquakes in Action* by Marianne Borgardt (Aladdin, 1993)
Pictures showing the devastating effects of earthquakes and volcanoes make this an excellent reference for flap books with a before-and-after theme. The reader looks at a house or forest before an earthquake or volcano and then lifts the flap to see the resulting destruction. After reading this book, kids can make their own before-and-after books about a natural phenomenon.

■ *What's Inside? Small Animals* (Dorling Kindersley, 1991)
This book is similar to a flap book in that it has photos of animals with their coverings peeled back to reveal their insides. Older children often enjoy making more detailed diagrams for their own flap books with ideas they get from this one.

Gift Book

What You Need

- several sheets of drawing paper (8$\frac{1}{2}$" x 11")
- lined writing paper (8$\frac{1}{2}$" x 11") or writing paper patterns on pages 84-85
- two pieces of tagboard for the cover (9" x 12")
- crayons
- felt-tipped markers
- pencils
- scissors
- glue
- ruler
- hole punch
- three loose-leaf rings (1" diameter)
- two pieces of ribbon (9" and 12" long)
- small press-on gift bow (optional)

What You Do

1. A gift book has a cover that is decorated to look like a present. You can make it to give to a friend or relative on any occasion. Write a story or poem and then think about how you would like to illustrate your book. You can make your own drawings, or glue in pictures or photographs. Make a first draft.

2. Check your work, make any changes that are needed, and create a finished copy. Put the pages in order. Make a title page and place it on top.

Gift Book

3. Decorate your front cover to look like wrapping paper. Punch holes at two inches, six inches, and ten inches down the left side of the cover. Glue the ribbons to the front cover, as shown. If you wish, add a press-on bow or make your own bow and glue it in place. Make a gift tag and glue it to the cover.

4. Using the front cover as a guide, punch holes in the back cover and inside pages. Line up all the pages and join the book together with the three loose-leaf rings.

Teacher's Corner

When your students need a gift for a relative or special friend, encourage them to create a gift book. These books are perfect for birthdays, Mother's Day, Father's Day, Grandparent's Day, or Valentine's Day. They are ready to give without wrapping.

■ *Fathers, Mothers, Sisters, Brothers—A Collection of Family Poems* by Mary Ann Hoberman (Little, Brown & Co., 1991)
This collection will give your students ideas for making their own gift books filled with original or copied poetry expressing their love for a relative. If they copy poetry, make sure they give the author credit.

■ *The Christmas House* by Ann Turner (Harper Collins, 1994)
This book contains poetry expressing the meaning of a family Christmas. These poems can be combined with drawings to make a lovely Christmas book.

■ *Families: Through the Eyes of Artists* by Wendy and Jack Richardson (Chronicle Press, 1991)
Some students may prefer to make gift books recalling special times spent with loved ones. This book will spark ideas for drawings and stories.

■ *Poetry Parade* by Pamela Klawitter (The Learning Works, Inc., 1987)
An excellent reference, this book contains illustrated instructions for writing quinzaines, triolets, triplets, creepy-crawlies, echoic poems, and more. It also includes a mini-book for students' poems that makes a perfect present.

■ *From Me to You* by Linda Schwartz (The Learning Works, Inc., 1995)
The thought-provoking questions in this book ask kids to write special memories and wishes for the person they are honoring. Includes original gift coupons, art, and poetry.

Hidden-Picture Book

What You Need

- two pieces of colored construction paper (9$\frac{1}{2}$" x 12")
- copies of coloring-book pictures or white drawing paper (8$\frac{1}{2}$" x 11")
- crayons
- felt-tipped markers
- stapler

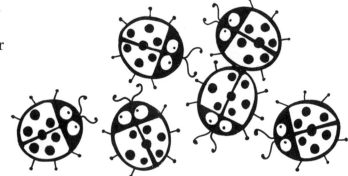

What You Do

1. In this book, you can draw a tiny creature hiding in a picture on each page. Your family and friends will have fun trying to find it. Think of a title for your book. It can be something like *Little Lost Ladybug*, *I Spy a Fly*, or *Where's the Worm?*

2. Draw your own pictures on white paper or choose the coloring-book pictures you like. Draw a tiny creature hiding somewhere on the page. Color all of your pictures.

Hidden-Picture Book

3. Decorate your cover and write your title on it. You can add a first page to show the reader what you have hidden in the pictures. Put the pages together and staple them into the cover.

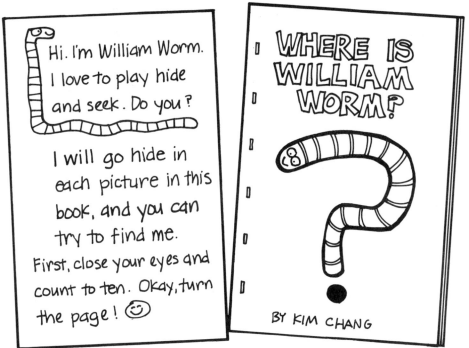

Hi. I'm William Worm. I love to play hide and seek. Do you?

I will go hide in each picture in this book, and you can try to find me. First, close your eyes and count to ten. Okay, turn the page! ☺

WHERE IS WILLIAM WORM?

BY KIM CHANG

Teacher's Corner

■ *Animalia* by Graeme Base (Harry N. Abrams, Inc., 1986)
This is a beautifully illustrated book with an alphabet theme. In each picture, there is also a hidden figure of a little boy. After sharing this book with your students, have them make a hidden-picture alphabet book to practice letters. Assign each student a different letter of the alphabet to hide in a picture. Have him or her print the letter neatly in the upper right-hand corner of the page as a clue. Arrange the finished pages in alphabetical order and staple them into the cover. Decorate the cover with different print fonts taken from magazines and newspapers. Write the title, "Look for the Letters," on the cover and put the finished book in your classroom library for everyone to enjoy.

■ *Have You Seen My Duckling?* by Nancy Tafuri (Greenwillow, 1984)
In this Caldecott Honor book, a mother duck loses one of her eight ducklings. For an interesting variation on the theme, have your students write a new story using another animal who has one of her children wander away.

■ *Where is the Bear?*, *Where is the Bear at School?*, and *Where is the Bear in the City?* by Bonnie Larkin Nims (Albert Whitman and Co., 1988, 1989, and 1992)
Children enjoy looking for the teddy bear in these books because of their appealing illustrations and rhyming texts. Have kids develop their own sequels. To help them think of ideas, you can suggest titles like *Where is the Bear in the Store?* or *Where is the Bear in the Zoo?*

The How-To-Make-a-Book Book
© The Learning Works, Inc.

How-To Book

What You Need

- several sheets of lined notebook paper ($8\frac{1}{2}$" x 11")
- several sheets of white drawing paper ($8\frac{1}{2}$" x 11")
- two pieces of colored tagboard for the cover (9" x 12")
- crayons or felt-tipped markers
- pencils
- scissors
- masking tape
- hole punch
- three loose-leaf rings (1" diameter)

What You Do

1. Use words and pictures to teach someone how to do or make something. For example, you can write a book on how to play a fun game or how to train a dog.

2. Decide what you want to write about. Plan the pages with headings and numbered directions. Write a first draft. Leave spaces for the pictures you want.

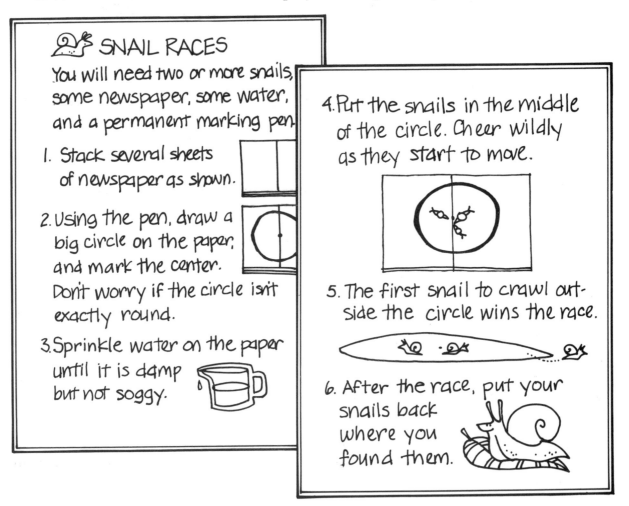

SNAIL RACES
You will need two or more snails, some newspaper, some water, and a permanent marking pen.

1. Stack several sheets of newspaper as shown.

2. Using the pen, draw a big circle on the paper, and mark the center. Don't worry if the circle isn't exactly round.

3. Sprinkle water on the paper until it is damp but not soggy.

4. Put the snails in the middle of the circle. Cheer wildly as they start to move.

5. The first snail to crawl outside the circle wins the race.

6. After the race, put your snails back where you found them.

How-To Book

3. Ask someone to read your directions to make sure they are complete and clear. Then write the final draft of your story. Draw pictures for your "how-to" book.

4. Make a hinged cover as illustrated with the Almanac (see step 5 on page 11). Punch three holes along the one-inch strip of the cover and the inside pages. Join the book together with the loose-leaf rings. Decorate the cover.

Teacher's Corner

How-to books give students practice in reading and following directions as well as organizing information in sequence. You can find many excellent how-to books written on a variety of subjects, including science experiments, art and music, games, pet care, and hobbies. Have students read how-to books on a variety of subjects before choosing their own book themes.

■ *Roald Dahl's Revolting Recipes* by Josie Fison and Felicity Dahl (Random House, 1994)
This contains recipes written in the same humorous style Dahl uses in all of his children's books. Kids can make cookbooks with their family's favorite recipes or recipes featuring foods of a particular country. Student recipes can also be combined into a group cookbook.

■ *Cat's Cradle* by Anne Akers Johnson (Klutz Press, 1993)
■ *Beautiful Origami* by Zulel Ayture-Scheele (Sterling, 1990)
Activities like string games and origami are popular with children and require limited supplies. These books provide illustrated, step-by-step guidelines for both.

■ *Let's Make Magic* by Jon Day (Kingfisher, 1991)
Magic tricks have widespread appeal. This is an excellent source for student books of magic tricks. Encourage kids to check the clarity and accuracy of their writing by carefully following their own directions to perform the magic tricks.

Invisible Pictures Book

What You Need

- several sheets of thin, white drawing paper ($8\frac{1}{2}$" x 11")
- two pieces of colored tagboard for the cover (9" x 12")
- pencils
- white glue
- black marker
- hole punch
- three loose-leaf rings (1")

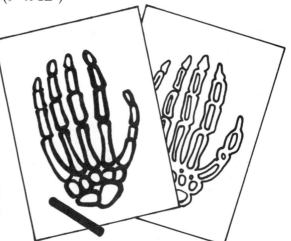

What You Do

1. This is a book of pictures drawn with glue. When the glue dries, the pictures are invisible. You can then take a piece of drawing paper and rub a crayon over the dried glue to have the outlines of your pictures appear.

2. Think of a topic for your book. Decide what words and pictures to put on each page. Draw your pictures with a pencil, then go over them with a black marker.

3. Place another sheet of white drawing paper over each page of drawings, being careful to line up the edges. Using a bottle of white glue, trace the pictures onto the white paper. It is best to use a new bottle of glue so that the hole is small and clean. When tracing, follow the lines of your original drawing as closely as you can. (You may want to practice tracing with glue on scratch paper.) Let your glue drawings dry overnight.

4. When the glue drawings are dry, write a story or the titles of the pictures on the pages.

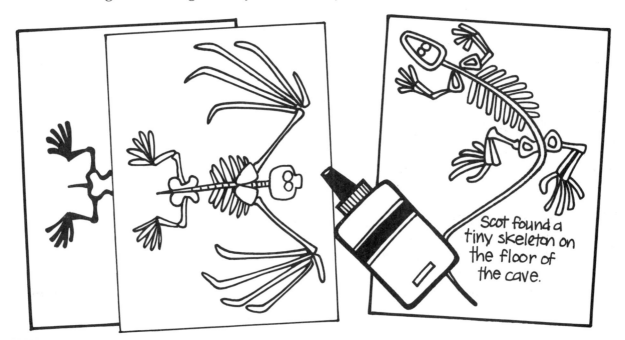

Scot found a tiny skeleton on the floor of the cave.

Invisible Pictures Book

5. On the inside of the front cover, write the following: "Directions: Place a clean sheet of paper over each page. Rub gently with a crayon."

6. Punch holes at two inches, six inches, and ten inches down the left side of the cover, as shown. Using this as a guide, punch holes in the back cover and inside pages. Decorate the cover and add a title.

7. Line up all the pages and join the book together with the three loose-leaf rings.

Teacher's Corner

Students can make invisible pictures for every page of their book, or use them as special effects to highlight one or two pages. Try this technique for spider webs, skeletons, or secret messages written in "invisible ink."

■ *Digging Up Dinosaurs* by Aliki Brandenburg (Crowell, 1981)
Dinosaurs are popular animals for the study of skeletons. Your students can make glue skeletons of their favorite dinosaurs using this book as a reference. Combine their glue skeletons with their written stories about dinosaurs to make a class book.

■ *Skeletons* by Jinny Johnson (Readers Digest Kids Books, 1994)
This is a good source of information about human skeletons as well as those of a variety of animals. Provide students with plain paper so they can make crayon rubbings of their glue skeletons once they have dried.

■ *Charlotte's Web* by E. B. White (Harper & Row, 1952)
■ *Anansi the Spider* by Gerald McDermott (Holt, Rinehart and Winston, 1972)
■ *The Very Busy Spider* by Eric Carle (Philomel, 1984)
These classic stories give students lots of creative ideas for their own books about spiders. Suggest they illustrate their work with spider webs made of glue. Provide clear pictures of actual spider webs for reference.

Mini Book

What You Need

- white drawing paper (9" x 12") cut into four pieces (4$\frac{1}{2}$" x 6")
- colored construction paper for the cover (5" x 6$\frac{1}{2}$")
- paper cutter or scissors
- crayons or felt-tipped markers
- scratch paper
- colored pencils
- stapler

What You Do

1. As the name suggests, mini books are small books. Think of a subject for your small book, such as words that begin with the same alphabet sound, or small animals, plants, seeds, or other things that are naturally small. Plan your story and write a first draft.

2. Decide how many pages you need for your final story. Each 4$\frac{1}{2}$" x 6" piece of paper becomes four book pages (front and back). Fold the pieces through the middle and staple them together with one staple. Carefully write your story on the pages. Add some colorful illustrations.

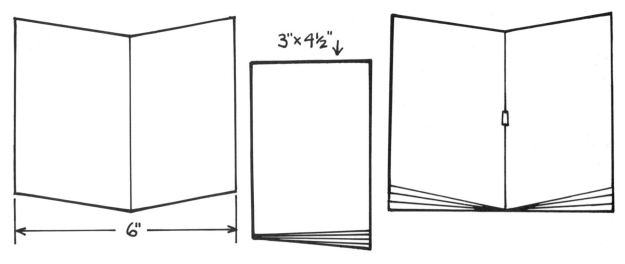

3" x 4½"

6"

Mini Book

3. Choose a cover for your book. Fold it through the middle. Write a title and decorate the front.

4. Line up the story pages inside the cover and staple them through the center, as shown.

Teacher's Corner

Mini books are quick and easy to make and can be adapted to a variety of teaching objectives. For example, young children can make a mini book about babies to practice words that begin with the letter "b." Start by having students brainstorm a list of "b" words related to babies, such as *bib*, *bottle*, *booties*, *bed*, and *buggy*. Ask them to illustrate and label one word on each page.

■ *Grandfather's Journey* by Allen Say (Houghton Mifflin, 1993)
Mini books can extend the theme of a book children have read or add details to the life or personality of the main character. Students can rewrite this story and include mini books to add information about life in another place. Their mini books can be glued to the back cover or hung freely like a bookmark from a length of ribbon attached to their main book. (See illustration.)

■ *The Tale of Peter Rabbit* by Beatrix Potter (F. Warne, 1902)
There are several books by Beatrix Potter originally printed in a mini-book format. Young children can draw small pictures of important events from this story and arrange them in a mini book. This will help them retell the story to their families. If they prefer, they can make a mini book of illustrations of their favorite Beatrix Potter characters, such as Jemima Puddle Duck, Tom Kitten, and Benjamin Bunny.

The How-To-Make-a-Book Book
© The Learning Works, Inc.

Mix-and-Match Book

What You Need

- several copies of the pattern on page 79
- two pieces of colored tagboard for the cover (7" x 8$\frac{1}{2}$")
- crayons
- felt-tipped markers
- pencils
- scissors
- stapler
- masking tape

What You Do

1. With a mix-and-match book, you can mix the parts of several pictures to make up new and unusual combinations. This book may be vertical or horizontal. Decide on a subject for your book. Choose something that involves large, simple drawings of people or animals.

2. Decide what to draw, and sketch your picture *evenly spaced* within the thirds of the page. For example, if you make an animal, draw the head in the first section, the body in the center, and the tail in the last section. Try to draw the animal parts the same width in each section so that when you mix and match, the individual pictures will cross the pattern lines at the same place, as they do in the illustrations below.

3. After you finish the drawings, color them.

Mix-and-Match Book

4. Make a hinged cover by cutting a $^3/_4$" strip off the long side of each piece of tagboard. Then join the pieces together again using masking tape. The tape will be on the inside of the completed book. (See illustration for step 5 on page 11.)

5. Stack the inside pages between the front and back covers. Staple the book together along the strip. Write a title on the cover and decorate.

6. Cut each picture into thirds along the lines.

Teacher's Corner

Before students draw pictures for their mix-and-match books, show them how the images in each section must cross the pattern lines at the same place in order for the books to work. You might suggest that students first make mix-and-match faces because these are the easiest to align.

■ *Making Faces* by Norman Messenger (Dorling Kindersley, 1992)
Students like creating all kinds of funny faces with this book. Have them make both individual and class books of unusual faces. They'll have fun adding details to the pictures. Explain that the eyes go in the top section, the nose in the center, and the mouth in the bottom.

■ *New at the Zoo* and *Have You Seen a Pog?* by Kees Moerbeek (Random House, 1989 and 1988)
These are mix-and-match flip books featuring zoo and farm animals and what they say and do. The pages are split in half and flip to create a number of unusual combinations. These books are fun to share with young children.

Older students often enjoy making their own "look inside" mix-and-match books, which complement the study of the human body. Students need four page patterns. On the first, they draw a self-portrait arranged in thirds. This becomes the first page of their book. On the next two pages, they trace two identical outlines of a body. (It is helpful if they have an outline to trace.) On the last page, they make the same body outline and draw the internal organs inside. This page remains uncut. The pages are then attached to a cover as in step 5.

Panorama Book

What You Need

- five to seven pieces of heavy, white drawing paper (9" x 12")
- two pieces of colored tagboard for the cover (6" x 10")
- clear tape
- scissors
- glue or glue stick
- crayons
- felt-tipped markers
- pencils
- masking tape
- stapler

What You Do

1. In a panorama book, you create a long scene that tells a story. Cut the drawing paper in half through the center so that the pieces are 6" x 9" long. Use clear tape to put the pieces together in a long strip.

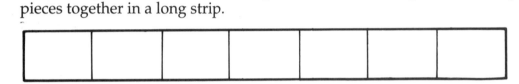

2. Think about where your story will take place. It could be anywhere—in a big city, in the ocean, at the circus, or on another planet. Write your story and plan out the drawings. Sketch your pictures so that the top edge has an interesting shape. (See the sample ideas illustrated below.)

3. Check your work. Finish coloring the pictures and cut away the top along the edge of the drawing, as shown. Fold the pages like an accordion.

Panorama Book

4. Make a hinged cover as illustrated with
    the Almanac (see step 5 on page 11).
    Decorate the cover.

5. Staple the two covers together. Glue the back page of your panorama to the inside of
    the back cover. The other pages should be free to fold out and stand up.

All day, the sky was full of clouds that
looked like scoops of ice cream. They
were pink and orange at sunrise.

Teacher's Corner

Panorama books combine the features of both shape and accordion books. Panorama books particularly appeal to students who excel in art and design because they provide an opportunity for the student to create an interesting visual display. Older students can also illustrate the front and back of each page.

■ *Where's Mouse?* by Alan Baker (Kingfisher, 1992)
This book is arranged with illustrations on both sides of the pages as well as peek holes to use when the pages are folded up. A simple text about a mother mouse looking for her baby accompanies the illustrations. Students can rewrite this story or create another version of it for their own panorama books.

■ *All the Places to Love* by Patricia MacLachlan (Harper Collins, 1994)
■ *Winter at Long Pond* by William T. George (Greenwillow, 1992)
■ *Greyling* by Jane Yolen (Philomel, 1991)
These books focus on setting and scenery; each can easily be adapted to a panorama-book format.

Peek Hole Book

What You Need

- several sheets of white drawing paper (8½" x 11")
- two pieces of colored tagboard for the cover (9" x 12")
- crayons
- felt-tipped markers
- scissors
- pencils
- masking tape
- stapler
- magazines

What You Do

1. In a peek hole book, you can peek through holes in the pages to see hidden pictures. Plan your story and pictures and the shapes of the cutouts for your peek holes. Large, simple shapes are the easiest to work with. You can either draw your own pictures or use ones cut out of old magazines.

2. Create a first draft.

3. Make any changes that are needed, recopy the story, and color the pictures. Cut out the shapes for your peek holes.

Peek Hole Book

4. Put the pages in order and fasten them together with one staple.

5. Make a hinged cover as illustrated with the Almanac (see step 5 on page 11). Add the title and decorate the cover.

6. Stack the pages between the front and back covers. Staple the book together along the strip.

Looking through the magic glasses, Luis suddenly had x-ray vision!

Peek-at-Me Book

What You Need

- several copies of the pattern on page 80
- two pieces of colored tagboard for the cover ($5\frac{1}{2}$" x $8\frac{1}{2}$")
- close-up photo of your face (photo will need to be cut; see film product package for safety warnings)
- crayons
- felt-tipped markers
- scissors
- pencils
- ruler
- glue or glue stick
- masking tape
- stapler

What You Do

1. This is a book all about you. When it's finished, you will see a different image of your-self on each page, but your face will always be the same. Think of a title for your book.

2. You need several copies of the pattern page. Cut your face out of the photo and glue it inside the circle on one of the pattern pages. This will become the last page of your book.

3. Plan your story and lightly sketch in the drawings to go with it. Cut out the small circles from the remaining pattern pages so that they reveal the picture of your face on the last page. Organize the pages and fasten them together with one staple.

Peek-at-Me Book

4. Check your writing and make any changes that are needed. Complete your drawings.

5. Make a hinged cover as illustrated with the Almanac (see step 5 on page 11). Decorate the cover and add the title.

6. Stack the pages between the front and back covers. Staple the book together along the strip.

Teacher's Corner

These books are fun to make and can provide a challenging exercise in problem solving. Simple books can be made in this format with blank cutout pages laid on top of a picture page. Kids can add text to the blank pages and decorate the shapes.

■ *The Secret Birthday Message* by Eric Carle (Harper & Row, 1972)
This is an excellent example of a peek hole book to share with your students. Shape pages are used in addition to the peek holes to add greater interest.

■ *Take Another Look* by Tana Hoban (Greenwillow, 1981)
■ *Look Again!* by Tana Hoban (Macmillan, 1971)
These books have photographs behind die-cut holes. Students see part of the picture, guess what it is, and then turn the page to find out the answer.

■ *Color Farm* and *Color Zoo* by Lois Ehlert (Lippincott, 1987 and 1988)
Share these books and examine their unique design with your students. Kids can then make their own versions using nine-inch squares of colored construction paper. Have them cut shapes from the center of the pages and align them carefully to discover animal faces.

■ *I am Special*, *Marvelous Me*, and *The Month-to-Month Me* by Linda Schwartz (The Learning Works, 1978, 1979, and 1976)
After sharing these books with your students, have them design their own books in which they express concepts of themselves. Using the format for the peek-at-me book, they can draw themselves in special costumes or as superheroes, for example. They will need a recent photo of themselves for the back page.

Personalized Book

What You Need

- several sheets of white drawing paper ($8^1/_2$" x 11") and lined writing paper ($8^1/_2$" x 11"), or writing paper patterns on pages 84-85
- two pieces of colored tagboard or construction paper for the cover (9" x 12")
- crayons
- felt-tipped markers
- pencils
- scissors
- masking tape
- hole punch
- 18" yarn, paper fasteners, or loose-leaf rings

What You Do

1. Rewrite your favorite story, making yourself one of the main characters. When you have completed the first draft, check your writing. Plan out any drawings you wish to include in your book.

2. Write your final draft and add the illustrations.

Jill and the Jellybeanstalk

Once upon a time in Tioga, Texas, there lived a girl named Jill who really, really, really liked jelly-beans. Her favorite snack was a peanut butter and jellybean sandwich. She ate jelly beans that were baked, boiled, frozen, or fried. She drank ice cold jelly bean juice.

Personalized Book

3. Make a hinged cover from tagboard or construction paper as illustrated with the Almanac (see step 5 on page 11). Punch two holes in the narrow strip on the front cover. Using that strip as a guide, punch holes in the back cover and inside pages.

4. Organize the pages of your finished book and secure them in the cover with yarn, paper fasteners, or loose-leaf rings.

Teacher's Corner

Students cherish the stories they create when they make themselves the main character. Chances are they have already imagined themselves as characters in some of the stories you've shared with them. Older students can rewrite stories to include friends as main characters, too.

■ *Danny and the Dinosaur* by Sid Hoff (Harper, 1958)
This classic is perfect for a personalized-book format. Kids can create new adventures where they either join or replace Danny in the story. In the latter case, their title might read *Linda and the Dinosaur*.

■ *Jack and the Beanstalk* by Steven Kellogg (Morrow, 1991)
Students often enjoy writing their own versions of this fairy tale, imagining themselves to be the giant, Jack, or the wife. Consider using other popular fairy tales of fables to prompt ideas for personalized books.

■ *Thomas' Snowsuit* by Robert Munsch (Annick Press, Ltd., 1985)
Students are sure to enjoy this humorous story, which is easily rewritten in a personalized-book format. They can write their versions to include friends as the teacher, mother, and principal.

The How-To-Make-a-Book Book
© The Learning Works, Inc.

Pop-Out Book
(Version A)

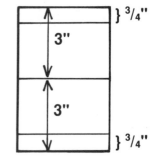

What You Need

- several sheets of white writing paper (8$\frac{1}{2}$" x 11")
- plain index cards (4" x 6")
- two pieces of colored tagboard for the cover (6" x 9")
- crayons and pencils
- masking tape
- felt-tipped markers
- glue or glue stick
- craft knife
- ruler

What You Do

1. Write a story. You will need one piece of writing paper for each page of your story. Think about how you can use pop-out pictures to tell your story.

2. Fold the writing paper in half and hold it as shown. Write part of your story on the bottom half of each page and illustrate each page.

3. Draw and color the pop-out figures on plain index cards. You will need one index card for each pop-out figure. Using a pencil and ruler, draw light lines on each card, as shown.

4. The $^3/_4$" strips will be glued to the pages of your book. Do not draw in those areas. Draw the main part of your figure in the lower large area. Draw the part that will stick up (such as the head or roof) in the upper area.

Pop-Out Book
(Version A)

5. Ask an adult to use a craft knife to cut around the part of each figure that will stick up.

✷ Allow at least a ¹/₂" margin here.

6. Carefully fold each card as shown. Glue the cards in place on the pages of your book. Let the glue dry.

7. Put all of your pages in story order. Carefully glue the pages back to back, taking care not to get glue on the pop-outs. Stand the book on its side to dry.

8. Use masking tape to make a spine for your book cover. Glue the first and last story pages firmly inside the cover. Decorate your cover and add a title.

Pop-Out Book
Version B

What You Need

- copies of the page pattern on page 81
- two squares of tagboard for the cover (5$\frac{1}{2}$" square)
- crayons
- pencils
- glue or glue stick
- scissors
- masking tape

What You Do

1. Write a story. Decide how many pages your book will have.

2. Cut out as many copies of the pop-out book pattern as you need. Fold each piece of paper in half with the dotted lines on the outside. Fold the curved part down to one side, folding it along the dotted diagonal line. Fold it down to the other side to crease it along that side of the diagonal line, as well. (See diagrams.)

3. Open each page out flat, with the blank side facing up. Write your story and draw pictures on the pages.

Pop-Out Book
Version B

4. When the pages are finished, push the diagonal folds to the inside so they will pop out when they are opened.

5. Stack the pages in order and glue them together back to back. Don't put any glue in the fold-out parts. Stand the glued-together pages on end to dry.

6. Use masking tape to make a spine for your book cover. Glue the first and last story pages firmly inside the cover. Decorate the cover and add a title.

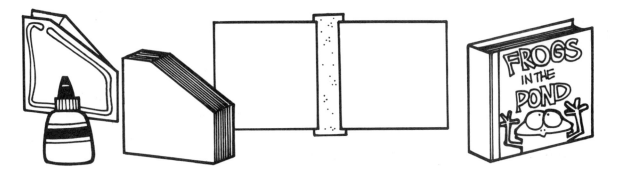

Teacher's Corner

Pop-out books are favorites with children of all ages. They are easy to make and can be adapted to most subjects. Here are some ideas for pop-out books your students can make.

■ *Vegetable Soup* by Jeanne Modesitt (Aladdin, 1991)
After you share this book, discuss what was in the soup. Assign each student a different vegetable to write about and illustrate. The vegetables can be illustrated on the pop-out portions of the pages. Assemble the pages into a book, and put a picture of children enjoying their vegetable soup on the last page. For variety, you can make a class book about different kinds of soups.

■ *Oh, My Fly!* by Jan Pienkowski (Price Stern Sloan, 1989)
It's fun for children to sing along as you flip through the pages of this book. Suggest that they make a book about their favorite song.

■ *Today is Monday*, illustrated by Eric Carle (Philomel, 1993)
Combined with Carle's pictures, the music makes this a delightful book for young children. Kids can remake it by writing about a food they plan to eat each day of the week. They can draw their food of choice on the pop-outs and include sing-along music on the last page.

■ *Zoo Doings* by Jack Prelutsky (Greenwillow, 1990)
Assign each child an animal to draw as a pop-out on a sheet of paper. Have the child write a poem about that animal, as well. Collect the students' work and combine their projects to create a class book.

45

Reversible Book

What You Need

- several sheets of white drawing paper (8$\frac{1}{2}$" x 11")
- two pieces of tagboard for the cover (9$\frac{1}{2}$" x 12")
- scissors
- masking tape
- pencils
- crayons
- felt-tipped markers
- stapler

What You Do

1. The text and pictures in this book illustrate opposites of a chosen theme, and are divided into two sections. After you read the first half of the book, you turn the book over and read the second half.

2. Decide on a subject for your book. It should be two opposite ideas, such as a city and country theme. You can write about other themes, too, such as day and night, winter and summer, or happy and sad.

3. Make a hinged cover as illustrated with the Almanac (see step 5 on page 11).

4. Insert the number of pages you will need between the front and back covers and staple in place along the hinge.

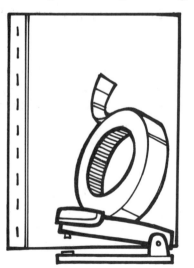

Reversible Book

5. Reserve half of your pages for the first part of your theme and the other half for the second part. For example, on the first set of pages, draw pictures of a car driving through the city and show the passing sights along its route. Add a story to tell about the trip through the city. On the last page of the city section, in the right-hand corner of the page, print the words "Now turn the book over and visit the country."

6. Turn the book over and draw pictures of the country on the remaining set of pages to show the places the car passes on its trip through the country. On the last page of this section, in the right-hand corner of the page, print the words "Now turn the book over and visit the city."

7. Decorate both covers to show the subject of the book when read in that direction. Add titles to the covers.

Teacher's Corner

■ *City/Country* by Ken Robbins (Viking Kestral, 1985)
Students read about a child who lives in the city and takes a car trip through the countryside. You can use photographs to help spark a discussion about your community—the homes, stores, parks, and businesses the children see each day. This book also enables students to think about other ways of life beyond their own community.

■ *Cinderella* by Russell Shorto (Birch Lane Press, 1990)
■ *The True Story of the Three Little Pigs* by Jon Scieszka (Viking, 1989)
These two books can be used to explain point of view. The first is written in the reversible-book format and can be read forward and backward as two complete stories. After reading either book, students can rewrite one of the stories from their own point of view, or, if they prefer, they can use the voice of one of the main characters in their version.

47

School Memories Book

What You Need

- several sheets of white paper (11" x 14")
- one piece of construction paper for the cover (12" x 18")
- scratch paper
- crayons or felt-tipped markers
- pencils
- stapler
- laminator (optional)

What You Do

1. Decide how many pages you want to include in your finished book. One sheet of the white paper will make four book pages (front and back).

2. Fold the sheets in half and number each page. This will help you keep them organized. Use scratch paper to plan your book and prepare a first draft with drawings.

3. Check your work and make any necessary changes. Color all of the pictures.

CAFETERIA CLASSICS!

PIZZA

SLOPPY JOES

CELERY WITH PEANUT BUTTER

COOKIES

MACARONI AND CHEESE

HOT DOGS

PUDDING

IDEAS
1. school song
2. cheers and mascot
3. teachers
4. other staff
5. special days
6. sports and games
7. clubs
8. classes
9. cafeteria
10.

School Memories Book

4. Use a piece of construction paper for your cover. Fold it in half. Write a title on the front of the cover and add decorations. Ask an adult to laminate it for you, if possible. Fit the cover around your finished pages. Attach the pages to the cover by stapling them together along the center fold.

Teacher's Corner

Allow students to work in groups of three to five to develop their memory books. Have them include interesting facts, such as the school address, the names of the principal and school secretary, and the size of the student body. You can suggest topics for them to write about, such as a favorite teacher, a best friend, a memorable school lunch, their most embarrassing moment, an after-school activity, or a team sport.

■ *Moving Up From Kindergarten to First Grade* by Chuck Solomon (Crown, 1989)
This book describes the sequence of activities in a typical school day. Young students might enjoy using this format for their school memory books. Help them begin by brainstorming a list of activities that are easy to illustrate. Have each student personalize the text by using his or her name in it. Another appealing theme for a memory book is a day that was special, such as a holiday or school awards day.

Older students can remember people or events that made the entire school year special. Have them make memory books during the last week of school as a way of encouraging them to recall the positive experiences they had during the course of the year. They can include pages for school photos and autographs.

Scrapbook

What You Need

- several sheets of white paper (11" x 14")
- two pieces of construction paper for the cover (12" x 15")
- pencils
- ruler
- white glue or tape
- felt-tipped markers
- magazines
- scissors
- hole punch
- loose-leaf rings
- laminator (optional)

What You Do

1. A scrapbook is a good place to keep small, flat items you want to save. Photographs, postcards, stamps, stickers, ticket stubs, menus, and award certificates can be kept in scrapbooks.

2. Punch holes at two inches, six inches, and ten inches on the left side of the cover, as shown. Using this as a guide, punch holes in the back cover and inside pages.

3. Cut out the letters of the word SCRAPBOOK from old magazines and glue them on the cover. Ask an adult to laminate the front and back covers for you, if possible.

Scrapbook

4. Arrange your scrapbook items on the pages, making sure to leave space where you have punched holes. Attach your items with glue or tape. If you wish, write a brief description below each item.

5. Stack your finished pages in order inside the cover. Using the three loose-leaf rings, fasten your book together.

Scrapbook Variation
Make a Diary

What You Need

- five copies of the diary pattern on page 78
- one piece of construction paper for the cover (8" x 10")
- pencils
- crayons or felt-tipped markers
- stapler
- scissors

What You Do

1. A diary is a book in which you can write about your personal experiences and thoughts. To make your diary, make five copies of the diary pattern on page 78 and cut them so that you have ten pages. Line them up carefully and staple in one place along the middle edge of the left side, as shown.

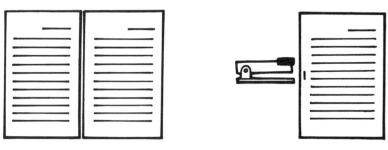

2. Fold the construction paper in half and print MY DIARY on the cover with crayons or felt-tipped markers. If you have access to a laminator, ask an adult to help you laminate the cover.

3. Fit your diary pages inside the cover and secure them with staples on the left side. Be sure to include the date on each of your diary pages.

Scrapbook Variation
Make a Diary

Saturday, Jan. 7

Dear Diary,
This was a cold, rainy day outside, but Jill came over and we had a great time. We worked on our scrapbooks, made taffy, and played with the kittens. Guess what — we have NO HOMEWORK this weekend! And Mom made spaghetti tonight. What a day !! ☺

MONDAY, MAY 16
I WON THE SPELLING BEE! MY "WINNING WORD" WAS <u>DIESEL</u>, WHICH I READ ALL THE TIME IN MY TRAIN BOOKS. TODAY I GOT THE SUMMER CAMP SCHEDULE — THERE'S A CANOE TRIP IN JULY THAT LOOKS AWESOME. TONIGHT WE HAD EXTRA SOCCER PRACTICE GETTING READY FOR SATURDAY'S GAME — THEN WE WENT OUT FOR ICE CREAM. JUST 18 MORE DAYS OF SCHOOL !!

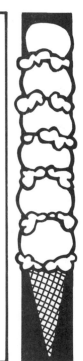

Teacher's Corner

These books encourage students to build and save personal memories, either with written accounts in a diary or tangible items in a scrapbook. The scrapbook is ideal for students who are too young to write in an actual diary. Older students can combine the diary and scrapbook formats or simply use the diary as a personal journal.

■ *Island Boy* by Barbara Cooney (Viking, 1988)
This is the story of Matthias Tibbets growing up, leaving for work, marrying, and returning to live on his family's island. Your students can assume the character of Matthias and write about what their lives might be like after returning to the island.

■ *Three Days on a River in a Red Canoe* by Vera B. Williams (Greenwillow, 1981)
Written in a diary/scrapbook format, this book is the account of a camping trip with a mother, aunt, and two children. It is easy to rewrite, but kids who camp can write about their own outdoor experiences.

■ *Carl Makes a Scrapbook* by Alexandra Day (Farrar, Giroux, and Straus, 1994)
The lovable Rottweiler, Carl, looks through the family scrapbook while taking care of the baby. The book contains scrapbook pages which serve as good examples of this kind of format.

■ *Marco Polo: His Notebook* by Susan L. Roth (Doubleday, 1990)
This interesting nonfiction reference contains a diary and scrapbook of Marco Polo's journey. Use it to encourage students to write their own books about explorers.

Scroll Book

What You Need

- one sheet of parchment paper or white shelf paper (12" x 24")
- pencils
- fine-tipped markers
- gold cord, colored yarn, or ribbon (18")
- watercolor paints (optional)

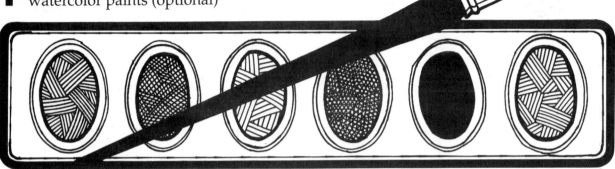

What You Do

1. Decide whether your scroll will read vertically or horizontally. Lay the paper in front of you in the direction you are going to write your story. Plan how your story will fit into the space that you have.

2. If you want your scroll to look old, carefully tear away the edges.

3. Lightly print your story in pencil. Sketch in your drawings.

Scroll Book

4. Check your work and make any necessary corrections. Finish the printing and the artwork with fine-tipped markers or watercolor paints.

5. Roll up your scroll and loosely tie it shut with a length of gold cord, yarn, or ribbon.

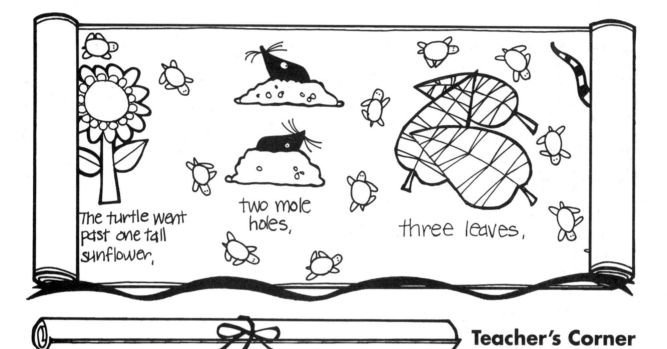

The turtle went past one tall sunflower,

two mole holes,

three leaves,

Teacher's Corner

Scroll books are a natural addition to the study of Asian cultures. They are easy to make and provide a fun alternative to the traditional book design familiar to children.

- *Grandfather Tang's Story* by Ann Tompert (Crown, 1990)
- *Lon Po Po* by Ed Young (Philomel, 1989)

These two books tell interesting stories in soft watercolors. The first is a story told with tangrams. (A tangram is a Chinese puzzle with five triangles, a square, and a rhomboid, all cut from one square. These can be combined in different ways to form a variety of figures.) The book also contains a tangram pattern that students can use to make animals for their stories. *Lon Po Po* is the Chinese version of *Little Red Riding Hood*.

- *The Red Thread* by Ed Young (Philomel, 1993)

The Chinese tradition of arranged marriages is explained in this story. A red line runs across the bottom of each page. If students write this story for their scroll books, they can use a needle and thread to stitch a line of red along the borders of their finished scrolls.

- *The Illustrated Gettysburg Address* by Sam Fink (Random House, 1994)

This book contains an interesting account of Lincoln's famous speech. After sharing this with your students, ask them to copy a paragraph of an important document, such as the Bill of Rights, onto a scroll. Older students can also use the scroll format to practice calligraphy skills.

The How-To-Make-a-Book Book
© The Learning Works, Inc.

See-Through Book

You will need to use a laminator and obtain help from an adult for this project.

What You Need

- several sheets of white drawing paper (8$\frac{1}{2}$" x 11")
- several sheets of lined writing paper (8$\frac{1}{2}$" x 11")
- two pieces of colored tagboard for the cover (9" x 12")
- crayons or felt-tipped markers
- scratch paper
- scissors
- pencils
- ruler
- masking tape
- stapler
- laminator

What You Do

1. Think of a story that involves things that can be looked through or looked into, such as a window, a television, a computer screen, or a magnifying glass.

2. Use scratch paper to plan where to include see-through portions. (For each pair of pages, make the see-through page first. Then create the "look-at" page that will follow it.) Carefully cut out and discard the see-through portion of the page. Place your drawing on top of a second piece of paper and sketch a picture in the hole you have created. Take away the top page and add to your drawing, if you wish. Color all of your pictures. Write a story to go along with your pictures. Repeat these steps for each page in your book.

He peeked through the keyhole...

And there was Bo- and a cake and presents!

See-Through Book

4. Ask an adult to laminate the see-through pages for you. Put all of your pages in order and secure them with one staple, as shown.

5. Make a hinged cover from tagboard as illustrated with the Almanac (see step 5 on page 11). Decorate the cover and add a title.

6. Staple the finished pages inside the cover.

Teacher's Corner

See-through books feature illustrations of windows, magnifying glasses, computer or television screens, keyholes, portholes, and other items that the reader can look through. Students enjoy drawing scenes behind the cut-out portions of the pictures. The see-through pages are laminated for durability.

- ■ *Windows* by Jeannie Baker (Greenwillow, 1991)
Ideal for nonreaders, this is a wordless account of the changes seen outside a child's window over the course of several years. Your students can make cutout window pictures of what they see outside their own bedroom windows. Individual pages can also be combined into a class book.

- ■ *Nature Spy* by Shelley Rotner and Ken Kreisler (Macmillan, 1992)
This book has close-up views of things in nature. Ask your students to make a cutout magnifying glass to view nature close-ups they have drawn.

- ■ *Ramona: Behind the Scenes of a TV Show* by Elaine Scott (Morrow, 1988)
Children often like to make television screens for their favorite shows. This story will give them ideas for making scenes from a Ramona book they have read.

- ■ *Beyond the Milky Way* by Cecile Schoberle (Crown, 1986)
The night sky often inspires creative drawings. You can use the engaging pictures in this book to teach a unit on constellations. Children can duplicate the scenes of a city sky at night for their own books. For more fun, have them include some close-ups by illustrating portions of the sky as seen through a telescope.

The How-To-Make-a-Book Book
© The Learning Works, Inc.

Shape Book

What You Need

- several sheets of white paper (8½" x 11" or larger)
- two pieces of colored tagboard for the cover (9" x 12" or larger)
- scratch paper (9" x 12" or larger)
- crayons or felt-tipped markers
- pencils
- scissors
- ruler
- hole punch
- loose-leaf rings (1")

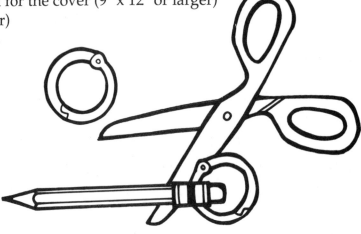

What You Do

1. A shape book has an interesting shape. You can tell what the book is about by looking at its shape.

2. Think of a subject for your shape book. Practice drawing a simple shape for the cover on scratch paper. Then cut your shape for the front and back covers out of tagboard.

3. Create a first draft of your story. Check your work, and decide how many pages you will need for your finished book.

Shape Book

4. Make pages for your book by tracing the outline of the cover shape onto white paper and cutting it out. Repeat this step for as many pages as you will need.

5. Write your story on the pages and add pictures.

6. Write the title on the front cover and decorate it.

7. Punch holes in the covers and pages. Line up all the pages and join them together with the loose-leaf rings.

Teacher's Corner

The shape book is an eye-pleasing format that appeals to children of all ages.

■ *Pizza All Around* by Dorothy R. Colgan (Parachute Press, 1992)
Create a wedge-shaped book of pizza recipes. Have students draw their favorite toppings on one side of a wedge and print a recipe for them on the other. Students can also design the book with new ideas for pizza recipes and/or information about the history of this popular food.

■ *Dinosaur Dream* by Dennis Nolan (Macmillan, 1990)
A larger format may be preferable for a shape book about dinosaurs. Students can cut the covers and writing pages in the shapes of their favorite dinosaurs and have their books open from the top. They can also use Wilbur, the main character in this story, to share factual information about their dinosaurs.

■ *Shoes* by Elizabeth Winthrop (Harper & Row, 1986)
Read this story in rhyme about all kinds of shoes. Suggest that your students make a shoe-shaped book with a variety of shoe pictures grouped by type. Students can also include shoe advertisements for math practice in price comparisons.

■ *Farming* by Gail Gibbons (Holiday House, 1988)
Young children can usually think of lots of farm activities and animals for barn-shaped books. *Farming* is an excellent reference because it has clear, simple illustrations that are easy for them to copy.

The How-To-Make-a-Book Book
© The Learning Works, Inc.

Slot Book

What You Need

- several sheets of white drawing paper (8$\frac{1}{2}$" x 11")
- two pieces of colored tagboard (9" x 12")
- one small piece of white or colored tagboard for puppet cut-out
- 3" piece of yarn (if making mouse puppet)
- craft stick
- craft knife
- masking tape
- scissors
- pencils
- crayons
- felt-tipped markers
- stapler

What You Do

1. This book has slots in the pages and cover that hold a small stick puppet you will make to go along with the book.

2. Think of your topic. For example, pretend there is a mouse in your house. Draw a mouse about two inches long on tagboard. (Make the outline of your mouse simple so it will be easy to cut out.) Color it, cut it out, and add a yarn tail. Attach it to a craft stick with masking tape.

3. Decide how many pages you want for your book. On each page, draw places in your house where a mouse could be, such as under a table, a refrigerator, or bed. Set your puppet on your drawings as you work to make sure it will fit, but do not draw a mouse in any of the pictures. Add a story to go with your drawings.

Miss Mouse tried to hide in a blue shoe.

Boffo flew past the bird bath.

The ants were all running after him!

Slot Book

4. Ask an adult to help you cut a slot with the craft knife in each page where you want the mouse to be. This will hold the mouse puppet. Add a piece of masking tape to the back of your slot to make it stronger.

5. Make a hinged cover as shown with the Almanac (see step 5 on page 11). Ask an adult to cut a slot in the book cover to store the mouse puppet when it is not in use. Decorate the book cover and add a title.

6. Assemble the finished pages in order. Staple the pages into the cover.

Miss Mouse looked out the window.

MISS MOUSE EXPLORES THE HOUSE
by Veronica Alvarez

MISS MOUSE EXPLORES THE HOUSE
by Veronica Alvarez

Teacher's Corner

■ *There's a Mouse About the House* by Richard Fowler (EDC Publishing, 1983)
This book has slots and comes with a movable mouse. In the story, the mouse runs around the house trying to avoid the family cat. Your students will also enjoy reading *Honeybee's Busy Day* by Richard Fowler.

■ *Mouse Views* by Bruce McMillan (Holiday House, 1993)
This book has photographs of a classroom pet mouse that gets out of its cage and explores the school. At the end of the story, there is a map of the mouse's path. With the ideas from this book, kids can make their own slot books about other adventurous characters. Have them include maps in their books, too.

Slot books featuring pictures of clothing make fun projects to accompany the study of weather, seasons, careers, and colors. Students can design book pages with various types of clothing corresponding to the study theme. Slots are cut at the necklines. Pictures of girls' and boys' heads are glued on craft sticks to insert into the slots. Kids can add text to explain the pictures. For example, they might write, "I wear a coat on a cold winter day" or "My dress is red." As students read, they can move the heads from side to side.

Step Book
Version A

What You Need
- one sheet each of blue, pink, yellow, and green paper (8$\frac{1}{2}$" x 11")
- two pieces of construction paper for the cover (9" x 9")
- ruler
- stapler
- crayons
- felt-tipped markers
- pencils

What You Do

1. Place the four pages on top of each other. Move each page over so that it is one inch from the page underneath it. (See diagrams.) Be sure the four layers are even.

2. Fold the layered pages over to form another four layers, as shown. You now have a total of eight layers.

3. Join the pages with one staple placed close to the fold.

4. Decide if you will use your book vertically or horizontally. You can write about tall things like trees, or turn the book the other way and write about long things like snakes.

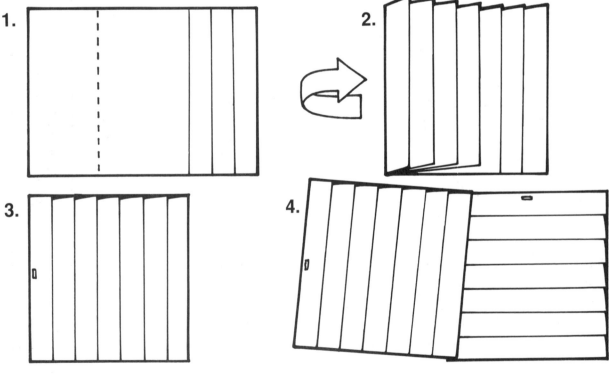

Step Book
Version A

5. Write your story and add drawings. Check your work and make any necessary changes.

6. Make a cover for your book using construction paper. Place the finished pages inside the cover and secure them with staples. Write the title on the front and add pictures if you wish.

Step Book
Version B

What You Need

- six pieces of colored construction paper (9" x 12")
- scratch paper
- scissors
- crayons or felt-tipped markers
- pencils
- ruler
- glue or glue stick
- stapler

What You Do

1. In this book, pages of different shapes are layered to form interesting pictures. Here are some ideas:

2. Decide what your book will be about and what shape each page will be. Use scratch paper to make a first draft and see how the shapes fit together.

3. Use the pages of your first draft as patterns to draw and cut out the pages of your book. Choose a different color for each page.

Step Book
Version B

4. Write part of your story on each layer. Use crayons or felt-tipped markers to draw details and add texture.

5. Make a cover using two pieces of construction paper. Write the title on the front, and decorate it if you wish. Put the pages between the front and back covers and staple your book together.

All was quiet in the camp.

Teacher's Corner

Both versions of step books can be used to practice classifying and sequencing. The time of day, months of the year, or days of the week make excellent subjects for sequential step books. Steps can be added by increasing the number of pages.

■ *Planting a Rainbow* by Lois Ehlert (Harcourt, Brace, Jovanovich, 1988)
This book has step pages with a variety of flowers arranged by color. Your students can make a similar book about vegetables.

■ *The Very Hungry Caterpillar* by Eric Carle (Philomel, 1969)
This book uses the step format to show the days of the week in sequence.

■ *Spooked!* by Keith Faulkner (Starlight Editions, 1992)
The art in this book features layered divisions of a single illustration. Older students can try this interesting variation of the step-book format.

■ *The Magic Schoolbus Inside the Earth* by Joanna Cole (Scholastic, 1987)
Students can use this captivating story with facts about the earth as a starting point for their own step books.

■ *The Great Kapok Tree* by Lynne Cherry (Harcourt, Brace, Jovanovich, 1990)
The author introduces children to animals of the rain forest that live under the kapok tree. Encourage your students to make their own step books about the rain forest.

Sticker Story Book

You will need to use a laminator and obtain help from an adult for this project.

What You Need

- several sheets of white drawing paper (9" x 9")
- two pieces of construction paper for the cover (9" x 9")
- removable stickers
- felt-tipped markers
- pencils
- ruler
- hole punch
- three loose-leaf rings (1")
- laminator

What You Do

1. This book has stickers that can be moved from page to page. They add to the pictures in your book and help to tell your story. Choose some stickers for your book and think of a story to go with them.

2. Decide how many pages will be in your book. Write part of your story on each page. Draw and color pictures to go along with your story.

Let's get on a bus and go to Sticker City.

There is a lot of traffic in the city!

We see many wonderful things in the stores.

3. Make a cover for your book with two 9" squares of construction paper. Write the title on the front and add pictures if you wish. Ask your teacher to laminate the cover and pages of your book.

WELCOME TO STICKER CITY

Sticker Story Book

4. Punch holes in your cover and pages, as shown. Line up all the pages and join the book together with the three loose-leaf rings.

5. Store your stickers on the inside of the front cover.

Teacher's Corner

This project requires a large supply of stickers. Ask each student to bring a package to share. The stickers are stored on the inside of the laminated front cover. Kids can put them in a scene and rearrange them as they like.

Try using some of these ideas for sticker-story book projects:

- Provide a set of nursery-rhyme stickers for students to match with a book of printed rhymes.
- Make a book of holiday backgrounds for students to match with appropriate holiday stickers.
- Have students match a flag sticker with a corresponding page of information on that country.
- Print research information about tropical birds, fish, or wild flowers. Have students read the text and match stickers with the information.
- Indicate the season and then have students put stickers of leaves, apples, or snowflakes on the branches of an apple tree.
- Provide colored happy-face stickers for students to match with color words. They can also match several stickers of one type to a corresponding number word. For example, they can put five apples next to the word *five*.

Texture Book

What You Need

- several sheets of cardstock or heavy white paper (11" x 14")
- scratch paper
- two pieces of tagboard for the cover (12" x 15")
- fabric scraps, ribbon, buttons, foil, plastic, cotton balls, felt, sandpaper, macaroni, newspaper, seeds, and other items to use for textures
- pencils
- crayons
- felt-tipped markers
- white glue
- scissors
- hole punch
- three loose-leaf rings (1")

What You Do

1. Choose a topic for your book. Then write a first draft of your story and sketch in your drawings.

2. Check your work and make any changes. Neatly copy your work to make a final draft. Color the pictures.

3. Decide where you can place textured items on your drawings. Choose the items you want and cut or arrange them into the shapes you need. Glue the textured items in place. Allow them to dry overnight.

The warm sand felt fine to Furbelow's feet.

She wore cozy mittens in the wintertime.

Texture Book

4. Design a cover using tagboard, and add your title. Punch holes at two inches, six inches, and ten inches on the left side of the cover. Using this as a guide, punch holes in the back cover and inside pages.

5. Line up all of your pages and join them together with the three loose-leaf rings.

Teacher's Corner

The texture format is particularly appealing to young children. On careful examination, they will find something in nearly every picture that suggests a texture.

■ *Runaway Bunny* and *Goodnight Moon* by Margaret Wise Brown (Harper & Row, 1942 and 1947)
This book uses cotton-ball bunny tails and aluminum-foil moons to enhance the retelling of these classic stories.

■ *Corduroy* by Donald Freeman (Viking, 1968)
To remake this favorite book, kids will need brown fur, green corduroy, and a small button.

■ *My House* by Lisa Desmini (Holt, 1994)
This book shows houses in a variety of textures. Students can design their own house textures using glue-on items. Then they can write descriptions of their creations explaining how their houses are unique.

■ *The Wartville Wizard* by Don Madden (Macmillan, 1986)
■ *Garbage!* by Evan and Janet Hardingham (Simon and Schuster, 1990)
These books open the way for discussions about trash and recycling. Your students can design their books from throwaway items they collect.

The How-To-Make-a-Book Book
© The Learning Works, Inc.

Time Book

What You Need

- several sheets of white drawing paper (8$\frac{1}{2}$" x 11")
- several sheets of lined writing paper (8$\frac{1}{2}$" x 11")
- two pieces of construction paper for the cover (9" x 12")
- pencils
- crayons
- felt-tipped markers
- ruler
- hole punch
- two 9" pieces of yarn
- clock-face rubber stamp (optional)
- calendar pages (optional)
- laminator (optional)

What You Do

1. Plan your story. Write about something that shows time passing, such as a day at school, a field trip, or a summer vacation. Your drawings should include clock faces or calendar pages.

2. Write a first draft of your story and add illustrations. Check your work and make any changes.

Time Book

3. Create a final copy and color the pictures.

4. Make a cover using construction paper. Write a title on your cover, and add pictures if you wish. Ask an adult to laminate the cover, if possible.

5. Punch holes at three inches and nine inches on the left side of the cover. Using this as a guide, punch holes in the back cover and inside pages. Line up all the pages and tie them together with the yarn, as shown.

Teacher's Corner

■ *My Cousin Kate* by Michael Garland (Crowell, 1989)
This book describes the activities of a young farm girl during a typical day. Students can compare her day to their own using pictures that include clock faces to show the passage of time.

■ *Time To* by Bruce McMillan (Lothrop, Lee and Shepard, 1989)
This book has photographs of a typical school day. Students can remake it with clock faces estimating the time of day.

■ *Zoo Day* by John Brennan (Carolrhoda, 1989)
Clock faces on each page of this book mark the time of day while on a visit to the zoo. Students can use a similar format as a follow-up to a field trip.

■ *Family Farm* by Thomas Locker (Dial, 1988)
■ *The Year at Maple Hill Farm* by Alice and Martin Provensen (Atheneum, 1978)
These books show the changing seasons and the passage of time in illustrations of farm life. Students can include both calendar pages and illustrations in their books.

Wheel Book
Version A

What You Need

- two construction paper circles (7" diameter)
- copy of wheel pattern on page 83
- scissors
- paper fastener
- crayons
- felt-tipped markers
- pencils

What You Do

1. Decide on a topic for your book. Select a topic that shows change or growth, such as a seed growing, an egg hatching, the ocean tides, or a sunrise or sunset.

2. Cut out the wheel and window patterns. Glue the wheel pattern to one of your construction paper circles. Poke a pencil through the dot in the middle of the wheel pattern to mark the center of your circle.

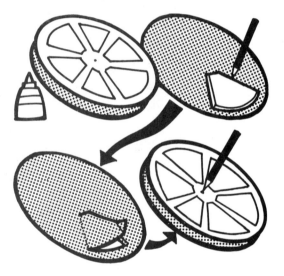

3. Place the window pattern on top of the other construction paper circle and trace around it, as shown. Cut out two sides of the triangle on your circle, as shown. Fold back the flap you have made. To make this flap easier to lift, fold back the corner. Place the other circle on top of your window circle and poke a pencil through the center of your window circle, as well.

4. The paper circle with the window will be the front cover of your book. Decorate it and add the title of your story.

Wheel Book
Version A

5. Your story will be told with a picture and short sentence in each section on the bottom paper circle.

6. Put the two circles together and join them through the center with a paper fastener.

7. Write and illustrate your story on the bottom circle. Include a picture and short sentence in each section, as shown. Working clockwise, complete the sections in order. To read the story, move the opening so that it lines up with the first section. Turn the top wheel to the right as you read.

Wheel Book
Version B

What You Need

- several sheets of white paper (8½" x 11")
- several sheets of lined writing paper (8½" x 11")
- two pieces of colored tagboard for the cover (9" x 12")
- tagboard scraps for wheels
- two to four paper fasteners
- crayons or felt-tipped markers
- pencils
- scissors
- hole punch
- ruler
- three loose-leaf rings

What You Do

1. Think of a wheeled vehicle—such as a car, truck, or bicycle—that you would like to illustrate. Create a front and back cover by sketching your picture on the large pieces of tagboard. (You may wish to draw your vehicle facing in the opposite direction on the back cover.) Color the covers and add a title to the front cover.

2. Cut wheels from tagboard scraps to fit your vehicle and attach them to your cover drawings with the paper fasteners.

Wheel Book
Version B

3. Write a first draft of your story and add drawings.

4. Check your work, make any changes, and create a final draft. Color the pictures.

5. Punch holes at two inches, six inches, and ten inches across the top of your cover, as shown. Using this as a guide, punch holes in the back cover and inside pages. Line up all of the pages and fasten them together with the three loose-leaf rings.

Teacher's Corner

Wheel books show change or movement in fun ways. Wheel books can also be made in a shape-book format combined with other special features, such as flaps and pop-outs.

■ *The Tiny Seed* by Eric Carle (Picture Book Studio, 1987)
This story explains the development of a seed. Your students can plant seeds and record the changes that occur in the sections of their wheel books.

■ *Traffic* by Betsy and Guilio Maestro (Random House, 1981)
■ *Bicycle Race* (Greenwillow, 1985); *Freight Train* (Greenwillow, 1979); *School Bus* (Greenwillow, 1984); and *Truck* (Greenwillow, 1980) by Donald Crews
These books are about moving vehicles. Kids will enjoy writing original stories about riding on a train, school bus, or bicycle.

Write-and-Wipe Book

You will need to use a laminator and obtain help from an adult for this book project.

What You Need

- several sheets of white drawing paper (8$\frac{1}{2}$" x 11")
- several sheets of lined writing paper (8$\frac{1}{2}$" x 11")
- two pieces of tagboard for the cover (9" x 12")
- felt-tipped markers
- laminator
- pencils
- scissors
- hole punch
- three loose-leaf rings
- small sponge or wash cloth
- overhead projector pen
- 24" piece of yarn

What You Do

1. This is a book of worksheets that can be used again and again. You write in the book with a special pen and use the sponge to erase your work when you are finished.

2. Think of an idea for your book. Tasks that require a minimum of marking and simple directions will work best.

3. Print the pages lightly in pencil and check your work. Trace over the printing and any pictures you have added with felt-tipped markers.

Write-and-Wipe Book

4. Decorate the cover and add a title.

5. Ask an adult to laminate your covers and inside pages. Cut out your laminated pages.

6. Punch holes at two inches, six inches, and ten inches on the left side of the cover. Using this as a guide, punch holes in the back cover and inside pages. Line up all the pages and join the book together with the three loose-leaf rings.

7. Securely tie one end of the yarn around the cap of the overhead projector pen and tie the other end to the center loose-leaf ring. Provide a small sponge or wash cloth for wiping the pages clean. (You may want to attach a plastic pocket to the inside of the front cover to provide a place to store the sponge or cloth.)

Teacher's Corner

Write-and-wipe books are easy to adapt to a variety of classroom activities. They are ideal for individualized instruction because their pages can be wiped clean and used again. Students can practice handwriting with a write-and wipe book. They can also create worksheet books organized by skill to use in the classroom learning center. Students enjoy making write-and-wipe books of story starters as well. They make these by printing the first sentence of the story on lined paper decorated with stickers. Then they give their books to friends or classmates, who complete the stories. Children can write several different story starters for popular themes, such as holidays, seasons, and birthdays.

- *Mouse Count* and *Mouse Paint* by Ellen Stoll Walsh (Harcourt, Brace, Jovanovich, 1989 and 1991)
- *Alphabetics* by Sue MacDonald (Macmillan, 1986)

Your students can make math and other concept books for themselves, younger siblings, or other classes. Reading these books will give them some interesting ideas for topics and layouts.

The How-To-Make-a-Book Book
© The Learning Works, Inc.

Diary Pattern

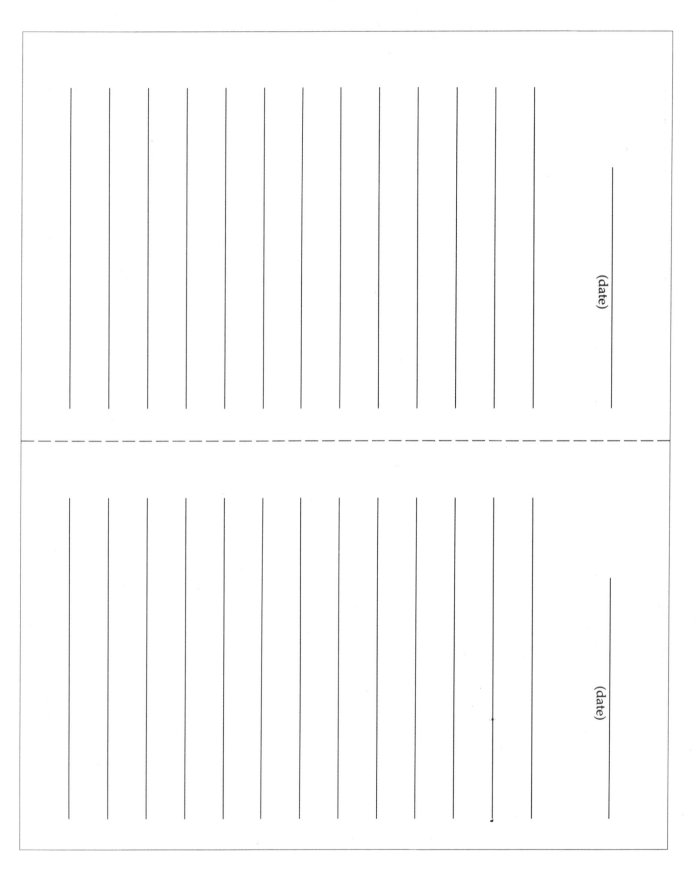

(date)

(date)

Mix-and-Match Pattern

Peek-at-Me Pattern

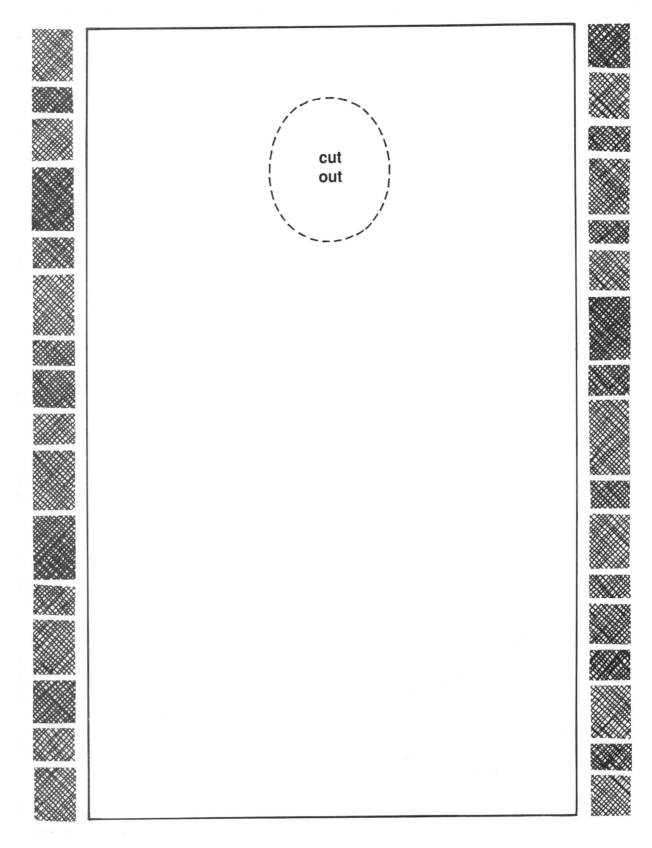

cut
out

Pop-Out Pattern

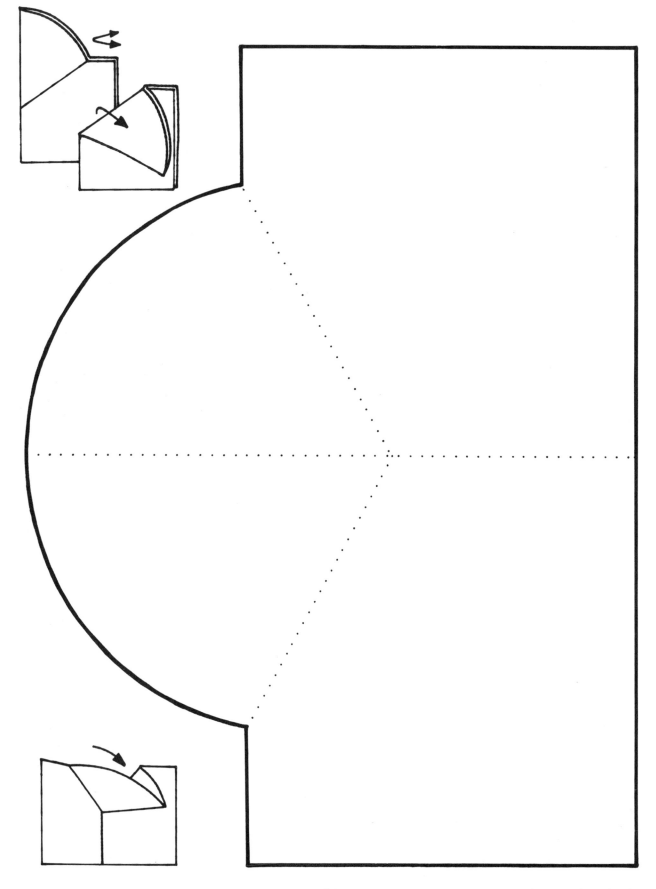

Train Patterns

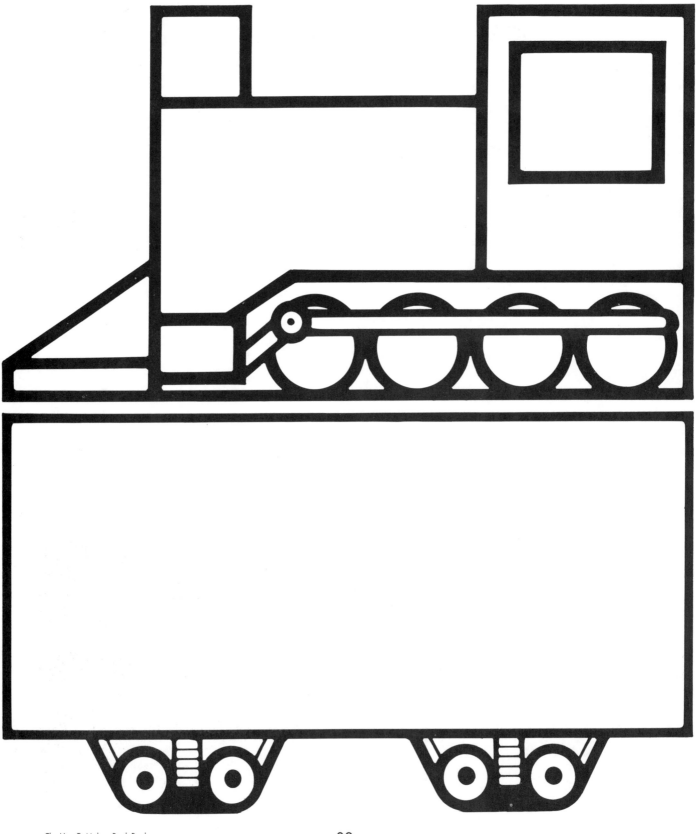

Wheel Pattern (Version A)

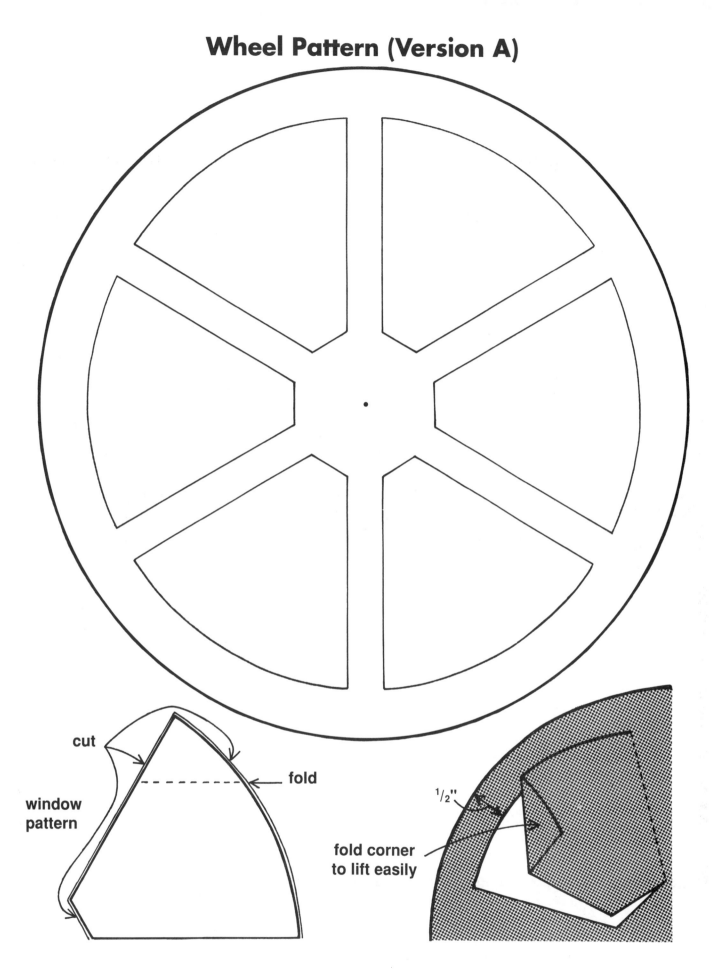

cut

fold

window
pattern

$1/2''$

fold corner
to lift easily

83

Writing Paper Pattern

Before copying this page, white out title, page number, copyright, and these instructions.

Writing Paper Pattern

Sample Books

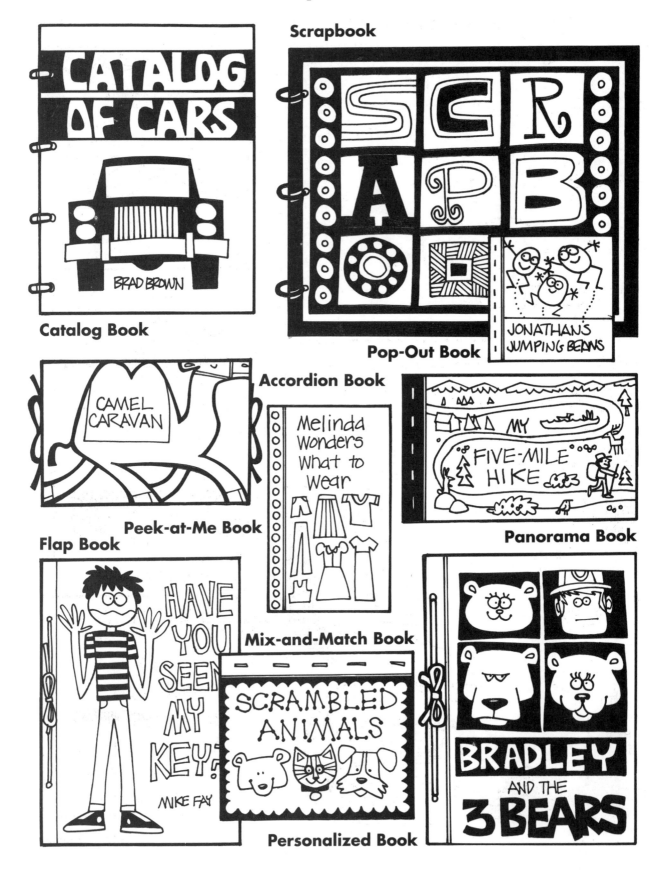

Catalog Book

Scrapbook

Pop-Out Book

Accordion Book

Panorama Book

Peek-at-Me Book

Flap Book

Mix-and-Match Book

Personalized Book

Sample Books

Texture Book

Shape Book

PICK A PUMPKIN
BY AMY CASEY

Slot Book

SLIPPERY, SCALY, FEATHERY, FURRY

LET'S TAKE A TAXI THROUGH THE TOWN
ONE WAY
LUIS LOPEZ

Mini Book

ITTY BITTY BUGS

WILD ABOUT WHALES
BY JOHN DOMMERS

HOW TO DRAW A TRACTOR

COUNTING CATERPILLARS
Darcy Daniels

Big Book

Wheel Book

Step Book

Publishers of Children's Writing

Here is a list of publishers who accept original children's stories, poetry, and artwork. You can find additional information in *Children's Writer's and Illustrator's Market*, F & W Publications, 1507 Dana Avenue, Cincinnati, Ohio 45207.

Children's Digest
Children's Better Health Institute
P.O. Box 567 Indianapolis, Indiana 46206-0567
800-558-2367

Highlights for Children
803 Church Street
Honesdale, Pennsylvania 18431-1824
717-253-0179

Jack and Jill
Children's Better Health Institute
P.O. Box 567B
Indianapolis, Indiana 46206-0567
800-558-2367

Kids are Authors Competition
School Book Fairs
801 94th Avenue North
St. Petersburg, Florida 33702
800-726-1030

Landmark Editions, Inc.
P.O. Box 4469
1420 Kansas Avenue
Kansas City, Missouri 64127
816-214-4919

Spark!
F & W Publications
1507 Dana Avenue
Cincinnati, Ohio 45207-1005
513-531-2222

Stone Soup
Children's Art Foundation
P.O. Box 83
Santa Cruz, California 95063
800-447-4569